101* WAYS

TO
RAISE
RESOURCES

by

SUE VINEYARD and STEVE McCURLEY

Brainstorm Series

Illustrated by Sue Vineyard

HERITAGE ARTS PUBLISHING
1807 PRAIRIE AVENUE
DOWNERS GROVE, IL 60515
(312) 964-1194

©1987 Sue Vineyard and Steve McCurley
ISBN 0-911029-05-2

All rights reserved. Any reproduction of material from this book must display credit to the authors and © information.

OTHER BOOKS BY THE AUTHORS:

"101 IDEAS FOR VOLUNTEER PROGRAMS", ©1986, Vineyard and McCurley
"Finding Your Way Through the Maze of Volunteer Management", ©1981, Vineyard
"Beyond Banquets, Plaques and Pins", ©1982, Vineyard
"Fundraising for Hospices & Other Groups", ©1983, Vineyard and Lund
"Marketing Magic for Volunteer Programs", ©1984, Vineyard

Published by:

Heritage Arts Publishing
1807 Prairie Avenue
Downers Grove, IL 60515
(312) 964-1194

INTRODUCTION

When our first book in The Brainstorm Series, "101 Ideas For Volunteer Programs" was introduced at VOLUNTEER's national conference in Dallas last year, strange things happened:

- All available copies were sold out in 4 hours
- People who had not gotten any of the supply were offering great sums and questionable "side benefits" to owners to purchase their copy
- The display copy mysteriously disappeared with $7 left in its spot
- People tried to steal the authors own copies from their brief cases
- Someone was seen photocopying an original

Because we are both quick and wise, we decided maybe we'd hit on something of value.

When asked what we planned to write next and we replied "Ideas on Fundraising", we noticed people were tearing at our bodies, begging us to hurry up and print it.

Being astute to such subtle suggestions we raced home to finish this, our 2nd in the series, and rush it to the printer, lest too many people try to steal our briefcases in search of copy.

To you we offer this book to use to tickle your own creativity and success in resource development. We hope you have as much fun using it as we had writing it.

Sue Vineyard
Steve McCurley
January 1987

ACKNOWLEDGEMENTS

This book is affectionately dedicated to all of the people who bought our last book and also decided to buy this one.

It is also dedicated to Denise Vesuvio and the Magic Macintosh, who made the whole thing easier, cheaper and a lot more fun.

Steve McCurley
Sue Vineyard
January 1987

TABLE OF CONTENTS

CHAPTER I.   **General Fundraising Advice**

1.	Great Ideas	8
2.	Basic Sources of Funds	9
3.	Better Word for Fundraising	10
4.	Pre-fundraising Questionnaire	11
5.	Statistics to Aid Fundraising	12
6.	Bad Fundraising Ideas	13
7.	Fundraising Objectives	14
8.	Fundraisers You Do Not Want to Know	15

CHAPTER II.   **Solicitation of Individuals**

9.	5 Step Plan to Major Gifts	18
10.	How to Ask for Money	19
11.	Ways to Acknowledge Donations	20
12.	Direct Mail Solicitation	21
13.	Components of Direct Mail Piece	22
14.	Drawbacks of Direct Mail	23
15.	How to Maximize Pledge Fulfillment	24

CHAPTER III.   **Corporations and Foundations**

16.	Contents of a Proposal	26
17.	Types of Corporate Support	27
18.	Avenues to Corporate Support	28
19.	Resources from Small Businesses	29
20.	Foundation Research Form	30
21.	Procedure for Making Foundation Requests	31
22.	Ways Not to Get Funded	32

CHAPTER IV.   **Utilization of Volunteers**

23.	Satisfactions to Appeal to for People's Involvement	34
24.	How to Manage Volunteers	35
25.	Rewards to Offer Volunteers	37
26.	Tips on Working with Volunteers	38
27.	Where to Recruit Volunteers	39

CHAPTER V.   **Non-Cash Resource Raising**

28.	Ideas for Cost Reduction	42
29.	Non-cash Donations	43
30.	Sources of Donated Services	45
31.	Sources for Donated Goods	46

© 1987. McCurley & Vineyard. 101 Ways.

CHAPTER VI.	**Special Events**		
	32.	Basic Rules for a Special Event	48
	33.	Goals for Special Events	49
	34.	How to Set the Date	50
	35.	Times Not to Schedule a Special Event	51
	36.	Pricing Tickets	52
	37.	What to Put on an Invitation	53
	38.	Special Event Themes	54
	39.	Piggyback Revenue Sources	56
CHAPTER VII.	**Publicity**		
	40.	Publicity	58
	41.	Ways to Promote	59
	42.	Qualities of the Publicity Chair	60
	43.	How to Get Publicity	61
	44.	Where to Get Free PR Help	62
	45.	Timeline for Special Event Publicity	63

CHAPTER I

GENERAL FUNDRAISING ADVICE

GREAT IDEAS

1. Publish a "Gifts Catalogue", listing all the goods and services that you would like to have donated to your cause. Either mail it to corporations and individual donors or ask a newspaper to run it as a page of donated advertising.

2. Construct an "Extended Budget" for your organization that includes the value of the donated volunteer time that is given your agency. Use this budget to demonstrate to funders that you have valuable community support that is 'matching' their donation of cash.

3. Build a fundraising solicitation team composed of three types of expertise: a staff member to answer technical questions and to appeal to the logic of the funder; a board member to demonstrate community support and to appeal to the power needs of the funder; and a service volunteer to demonstrate the actual work of the program and to appeal to the emotions of the funder.

4. Investigate "negative fundraising". Explore all the ways that you can save money, either by reducing your expense by getting direct donations of goods and services or by engaging in cost-sharing purchasing arrangements.

5. Think of fundraising as a long-term effort. Begin now to establish a 'donors listing' that will form the base of your solicitation market in years to come. Keep listings of all your clients, all attendees at special events, and all others who come into favorable contact with your organization.

6. Never plan a special event at which you are trying to raise money that does not piggyback several potential sources of revenue. Do not try to make money off the initial ticket price alone, because there is a direct conflict between the size of the potential attending audience and the cost of the ticket.

7. Whenever you plan to make a corporate solicitation, try to develop some specific statistics about the extent to which you directly serve the employees of that corporation. Compile statistics or examples of projects that relate to the corporation and its people, either those who are your clients or those who volunteer for you.

8. Keep your eyes open for "The Story", a great anecdote that will poignantly demonstrate the need for your agency. A good story, like a good picture, is worth a thousand statistics.

9. Remember that step one of effective fundraising may be getting the right people on your board of directors.

10. Since it is easier to get donated goods and services than money from corporations, approach them with a "Chinese menu" that will allow you to take any of the three types of contributions. Then, after you have demonstrated what great use you have made of their donated goods and services, use this track record to ask for cash.

© 1987. McCurley & Vineyard. 101 Ways.

BASIC SOURCES OF FUNDS

1. Telethon
2. Direct Mail
3. Special events
4. Individual donations
5. Bequests
6. United Way
7. Ad book sales
8. Combined Federal Campaign
9. Corporate donations
10. Foundation grants
11. Investments
12. Income from business subsidiary
13. Gifts and civic and service clubs
14. Door-to-door campaigns
15. Memorial fund
16. Coin cans
17. Fountain throw
18. Sale of merchandise
19. Donor option funds
20. Corporate matching gifts
21. Life insurance
22. Endowment fund
23. Auctions
24. Corporate foundation grants
25. Government contracts
26. Fees for service
27. Church fund
28. Bingo
29. Membership fees
30. Special membership assessment
31. Designated percentage of fines
32. Donations from fraternals
33. Donations from business and professional associations
34. Revenue sharing allocation
35. Phone-a-thon

© 1987. McCurley & Vineyard. 101 Ways.

BETTER WORD FOR FUNDRAISING

PRE-FUNDRAISING SELF-ANALYSIS QUESTIONNAIRE

1. What is your agency's mission? What are you trying to accomplish? How would you explain your purpose in 25 words or less?

2. Who are your clients? Who do you serve? Who else benefits from this service - family members or employers of clients? Who don't you serve and why?

3. What geographic areas do you serve?

4. Who else does what you do or could be confused with you?

5. How are you different from each of these groups?

6. Do you have a long-range organizational plan? Is it tied to short-term project plans? Are these plans the basis for your fundraising or are you just chasing money?

7. Does your agency have a well-developed budgeting and accounting system?

8. What are your current sources and amounts of funding? Do these represent restricted or unrestricted funding?

9. What non-cash resources does your agency receive?

10. What previous experience do staff and board members have at fundraising?

11. What amounts of funding are needed? What type of funding is being sought: general support or project funding? What is the timeframe for developing new funding?

12. What resources can be allocated to fundraising: cash, staff, and board?

© 1987. McCurley & Vineyard. 101 Ways.

STATISTICS TO AID FUNDRAISING

1. Percentage raised that goes directly to aid clients.

2. Number of clients served.

3. Number of volunteers in program.

4. Number and value of volunteer hours contributed.

5. List of current funders.

6. Percentage of self-generated revenue.

7. Favorable changes in funding pattern over the years.

8. Extent of free care to needy community members.

BAD FUNDRAISING IDEAS

1. Anything that endangers participants.

2. Anything that's been done to death.

3. Poorly organized events.

4. Trying to raise money when it's not needed.

5. Trying to force an idea down the throats of others.

6. Trying to raise money for a non-perceived need.

7. Events associated with previous bad history.

8. Appeals based on misinformation, conning, or guilt.

9. Appeals which invade the privacy or dignity of clients.

© 1987. McCurley & Vineyard. 101 Ways.

FUNDRAISING OBJECTIVES

1. Raise money.

2. Create awareness of agency cause, etc.

3. Gather more volunteers to the ranks.

4. Gather new ideas for future programs.

5. Solidify credibility in community.

6. Educate public.

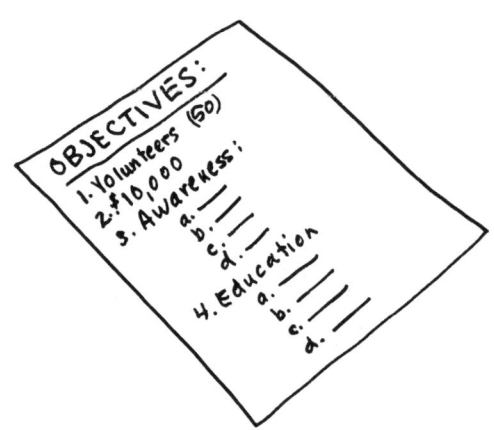

FUNDRAISERS YOU DO NOT WANT TO KNOW!

© 1987. McCurley & Vineyard. 101 Ways.

© 1987. McCurley & Vineyard. 101 Ways.

CHAPTER II

SOLICITATION OF INDIVIDUALS

5 STEP PLAN TO GET MAJOR GIFTS

1. Identification
   a. Identify those people capable of making large gifts to your organization
   b. Create a list of individuals most likely to give
   c. Research this list to determine likes, habits, patterns of giving, motivations, contacts you share, authenticators you already know or have involved, etc.

2. Education
   a. Choose best ways to tell prospective donors about you
   b. Get your story out every possible way: newsletter, public speaking, PR campaign, cocktail party gossip, etc.

3. Cultivation
   a. Win their hearts!
   b. People either give because they get something they need/want (tangible or intangible) or in commitment to the asker or the cause
   c. Establish personal contact
   d. Talk to someone who knows them to learn more about them
   e. Be honest, up-front caring
   f. Tell them what's in it for them
   g. Tell them what your commitment is
   h. Help them feel comfortable in giving

4. Solicitation
   a. Ask one on one
   b. Ask specifically for what you want
   c. Be brief, courteous, and positive
   d. Listen carefully
   e. Diagnose objections and remove them
   f. Ask for clients served, not the organization

5. Appreciation
   a. Write a handwritten note of thanks
   b. Know what additional type of thank you or reward would be appreciated
   c. Keep them informed during the year as to what this money has accomplished
   d. Make them feel part of the organization's success

© 1987, McCurley & Vineyard, 101 Ways.

HOW TO ASK FOR MONEY

1. Make a contribution yourself first
2. Ask in person
3. Do your homework about the funding source
4. Do your homework on your organization
5. Practice your pitch
6. Tell the truth, don't exaggerate
7. Stress the cause, not the organization
8. Never promise what you can't deliver
9. Tell, don't sell
10. Have your facts in order
11. Take written materials for people who are 'readers'
12. Show financial picture in pie chart form
13. Take "authenticator" with you to give you credibility
14. Have mutual friend make the appointment
15. Keep eye contact direct
16. Ask for people served, not the fundraising effort itself
17. Start by linking the people served to your cause
18. Tell why you are involved/committed
19. Never use quarter words when nickel words will do
20. Diagnose any objections and work to remove them, but if you don't know an answer don't make it up.
21. Don't try to talk them into saying 'yes'; remove their reasons to say 'no'.
22. Ask specifically - "hinting" will not work
23. Avoid putting other groups and causes down
24. Avoid 'ball-out' pleas. No one likes to support a sinking ship.
25. Meet the donor's need for information, reassurance, etc.
26. Paint a picture of what their help will mean in terms of people helping
27. Be yourself

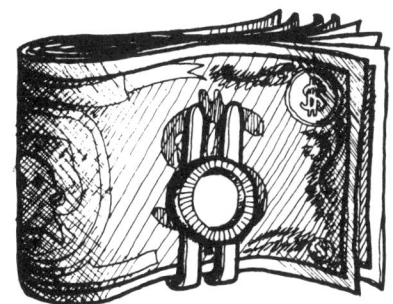

© 1987. McCurley & Vineyard. 101 Ways.

WAYS TO ACKNOWLEDGE DONATIONS

1. Thank you letter
2. In person thank you
3. Annual funders' listing in newsletter
4. Put on mailing list to receive materials, newsletters, etc.
5. Acknowledge in all PR
6. Name something after them: "The George Philpot Memorial Coffee Machine"
7. Send tax deduction verification letter
8. Tell them what you accomplished with the money
9. Give them a receipt
10. Get an article put in the newspaper about them
11. Send a letter to their boss
12. Send a letter to their family
13. Buy them a small personal gift of little value but of great charm
14. Make them an honorary member of your organization
15. Put their name on a plaque with other Great Givers
16. Give them display booths at your meetings
17. List them in your annual report
18. Send a Letter to the Editor about them
19. Nominate them for an award

DIRECT MAIL SOLICITATION

1. Direct-mail is not magic and can be expensive. It must be done carefully and well if it is to succeed.

2. Charities with 10 members ought to try something besides direct mail.

3. Start by collecting all the funding appeals that you receive in the mail. Analyze what you like and dislike about each. Adopt the good points to your own need.

4. Test each piece before you mail it. Try different types of enclosures and messages with different mailing lists.

5. Concentrate on the area of greatest agreement in your audience.

6. Find a theme that few could disagree with and hammer it home.

7. Use attractive graphics with strong wording.

8. Concentrate on achievement - what will be done with the money - and accomplishment, not just on need.

9. Use simple, direct wording.

10. Appear hopeful, not hopeless - people don't give money to lost causes.

11. Utilize a personal approach: address the potential donor as an individual; have the letter written on a person-to-person basis; talk about the problem in individual, not mass, terms.

12. Convey a sense of urgency, not panic. Be Paul Revere, not Chicken Little.

13. Tell how much you want and why this is a fair share for them to contribute.

14. Plead the cause, not the organization.

15. Be daring rather than bland.

16. Count on having to do several follow-up letters.

17. Tell people how to respond: who to make check out to and how to return it.

18. Note, but don't overstress, tax deductibility.

COMPONENTS OF A DIRECT MAIL MARKETING PIECE

1. Response or Gift Card
   a. This is the most important piece in the mailing.
   b. It should stand out from the rest of the mailing.
   c. Use large type on one side only.
   d. Involve the reader by using check boxes and "Yes" statements that encourage several different levels of giving.
   e. If possible, put the recipient's name and address on the card.
   f. Make all other parts of the mailing lead to the card.

2. Outside Envelope
   a. Ideally, this should look like a personal letter, individually addressed, with a postage stamp.
   b. Less effective and expensive, is to make the letter look like a 'bill', utilizing a window envelope.
   c. Avoid the standard size business envelope.
   d. Use warm colors like ivory or beige.
   e. Check with the post office for their size regulations before purchasing my envelopes.
   f. Avoid teaser copy on the outside - it brands it as 'junk mail.'

3. Return Envelope
   a. Use business reply mail.
   b. Use warm colors and nonstandard size.
   c. Teaser copy here can stimulate response.

4. Cover Letter
   a. Should tell reader what rest of mailing consists of.
   b. Mention response card 3 times.
   c. Ask for contribution in 1st paragraph.
   d. Talk about specific cases rather than your general purpose.
   e. Use non-standard sized stationary.
   f. Use ink other than black or blue.
   g. Use special letterhead for mailing.
   h. Have letters typed on automatic typewriter for individualized look.
   i. Long letters are all right if well written. They must make the same point over in as many different ways as possible.
   j. Shorter is better for the beginner.

5. Brochure
   a. Use only if it says the 'right' things. It could force the reader to find things he disagrees with you about.
   b. Consider including interviews with donors.
   c. Use photos that stimulate involvement.
   d. Use a story of a client helped.
   e. Consider using a "test" that readers can easily pass.
   f. Include information that readers can use.

© 1987. McCurley & Vineyard. 101 Ways.

DRAWBACKS OF DIRECT MAIL SOLICITATION

1. It yields good returns only when utilized on a massive basis. A 2% response is considered good.

2. It does not persuade. Your best response will come from people who already agree with you.

3. It is expensive and time-consuming.

4. It will offend some of the people who are solicited and generate a negative image of your organization and your cause.

5. It is unpredictable.

6. It is increasingly very competitive.

7. It generally nets only small gifts.

8. No direct mail piece works all the time. You will have to continually develop new themes and appeals.

9. You need to continually develop new prospect listings to solicit.

HOW TO MAXIMIZE PLEDGE FULFILLMENT

1. Remember that your goal is to convert occasional givers into regular donors with regular and recurrent giving habits.

2. Let pledger know that he/she is a vital partner in the work of the agency:
   a. When they pledge, insure they know they are a part of a group of supporters undertaking a specific challenge
   b. Help pledger know they are being counted on by <u>clients</u>
   c. Develop close relationship with pledger
   d. Keep them well informed of their group status
   e. Help pledger see vision of what can be accomplished with their help
   f. Insure their understanding that their gifts are essential in order to provide steady, dependable source of income to help clients
   g. Give pledge program unique name that signifies its purpose and ties it to work of parent organization
   h. Include good information in monthly appeal mailing that appeals to their involvement
   i. Have personalized information: name address, etc.
   j. Don't make appeals too slick - suggest frugality without cheapness
   k. Supply a return envelope with request

3. Treat the pledger in a serious, business-like manner
   a. Relate to pledger in good faith - take their word seriously
   b. Handle their pledge in a straightforward way
   c. Call your monthly effort a 'Pledge Fulfillment" or "Pledge Statement' to remind them of their commitment
   d. Remind pledgers if they fall delinquent

4. Emphasize the voluntary nature of the pledger's commitment
   a. Make reference to donor's goodwill and voluntary participation
   b. Tell them how much you appreciate them and need their gifts
   c. Have pledge statement carry reminder of their pledge and how it is helping to accomplish overall good

5. Constantly reaffirm the wisdom and value of the donor's commitment to pledge monthly contributions
   a. Instill a sense of well-being and personal fulfillment concerning the donor's decision to make a pledge - reinforce this monthly
   b. Tell what your organization has been able to do because of their contribution - create a 'Band Wagon' feeling
   c. Offer special reports on unique projects
   d. Have appeals reflect the immediacy of your need

CHAPTER III

CORPORATIONS AND FOUNDATIONS

CONTENTS OF A PROPOSAL

1. Executive Summary: brief program description and budget total

2. Statement of need: analysis of problem area. Make this specific to your geographic area.

3. Project description: what will be done and what it will accomplish.

4. Organizational description: history, board list, expertise in area, indications of community support.

5. Timeline for project.

6. Staffing requirements and qualifications.

7. Budget

8. Proof of tax exempt status

9. Evaluation plan

10. Dissemination plan

11. Future funding plans

© 1987. McCurley & Vineyard. 101 Ways.

TYPES OF CORPORATE SUPPORT

1. Donate equipment or supplies
2. Allow charitable solicitation on premises
3. Put publicity in corporate newsletter
4. Allow use for corporate facilities for meetings, events
5. Sell fundraiser tickets to employees
6. Lend use of AV facilities
7. Provide free office space
8. Donate products to use as prizes
9. Loan PR help
10. Encourage employees to volunteer
11. Allow to use postage meter
12. Give access to telephones
13. Print brochure
14. Assign a high level board member
15. Match employee donations
16. Give a corporate contribution
17. Piggyback purchase of supplies and equipment
18. Introduce to other businesses
19. Provide artistic design assistance
20. Buy corporate table at fundraiser
21. Allow agency to set up information booth on corporate premises
22. Refer employees who need help to agency
23. Allow payroll deduction contributions
24. Donate a vehicle
25. Donate board meeting space
26. Piggyback advertising
27. Sponsor a newspaper ad
28. Recognize employees who volunteer
29. Talk about volunteering in pre-retirement seminars
30. Buy agency products
31. Chair a special event fundraiser
32. Adopt a agency
33. Do their accounting
34. Maintain mailing list on computer
35. Print newsletter

© 1987. McCurley & Vineyard. 101 Ways.

AVENUES TO CORPORATE SUPPORT

1. Through employee volunteers to matching gifts program
2. Request to corporate contributions department
3. Request to corporate foundation
4. Joint marketing proposal to PR department
5. Request to department heads for assistance on projects
6. Request to plant and store managers for donated products
7. Request to office manager for surplus equipment
8. Request to advertising department for new products
9. Through union for joint union/management project
10. Through retirees
11. Directly to employees to participate as volunteers
12. Through a board member who works at the corporation
13. Through employee volunteer team recruited for a fundraising

© 1987. McCurley & Vineyard. 101 Ways.

RESOURCES FROM SMALL BUSINESSES

1. Placement of coin cannisters

2. Placement of posters in windows

3. Prizes for events:
    a. certificate from ice cream store
    b. coupons from fast food restaurants
    c. movie tickets
    d. free bottle of wine
    e. subscription to community newspaper
    f. free fill-up of gasoline
    g. free bag of groceries
    h. use of limousine for a week
    i. case of soft drinks or beer
    j. photo of family
    k. free watch cleaning
    l. month at exercise salon
    m. free pass at amusement park
    n. weekend stay in hotel
    o. beauty parlor appointment
    p. floral arrangement

4. Site for outdoor meeting at golf course, farm.

FOUNDATION RESEARCH FORM

1. Name of foundation: _____
2. Address: _____
   _____
3. Phone: _____
4. Current assets: _____
5. Last year's grant total: _____
6. Average size of grant: _____
7. Grant size range: _____
8. Subject area of giving: _____
9. Geographic limitations: _____
10. Other limitations: _____
11. Names, affiliations of foundation board: _____
12. Format for presentations: _____
    a. Program officer
    b. Size limitations, format
    c. Number of copies
13. Timing of solicitations: _____
14. Timing for decisions: _____
15. People associated with you who can act as contacts: _____
16. Your previous history with the foundation: _____

© 1987. McCurley & Vineyard. 101 Ways.

PROCEDURE FOR MAKING A REQUEST FROM A FOUNDATION

1. Do background research on the foundation to determine their policies and procedures.

2. Try to get to know the foundation staff. Do this either formally (ask for a meeting) or informally (at meetings, parties, conferences, etc.).

3. Arrange a formal meeting to discuss ideas and possibilities. Have a concrete project in mind before you meet. Don't press for a commitment at this meeting, just for an opportunity to continue.

4. Place the foundation staff on your mailing list to receive material about your organization.

5. Prepare a proposal along the foundation's desired format. Personalize the proposal for the foundation and include a personalized cover letter. Include a summary if the proposal is complex or lengthy. Indicate that you are available to discuss the proposal and answer questions, and that you will follow-up with a phone call in a few weeks.

6. Follow-up with a courtesy call. Be discreet. Do not press, but appear helpful and ready to answer questions.

7. If you do not get funding, try to determine whether the difficulty was one of subject area, approach, technique, etc. Attempt to correct difficulty and re-approach the foundation. Do not get angry and don't take the rejection personally.

8. If you do get funding, write a thank you note. Continue to provide reports to the foundation on significant accomplishments.

© 1987. McCurley & Vineyard. 101 Ways.

WAYS NOT TO GET FUNDED

1. Fail to read this list
2. Mis-spell funder's name
3. Look sloppy in your approach
4. Assume you're "owed" funding
5. Make unreasonable time demands
6. Be bland: become the lowest common denominator
7. Focus only on raising money, not resources
8. Try to scare the donor into giving
9. Try to make the potential donor feel guilty
10. Assume your funders don't know what you're really doing
11. Don't know your own facts
12. Try to con your funder
13. Don't do your homework about them
14. Forget to ask for the money
15. Beg
16. Be late for your appointment
17. Drone on beyond your allotted time
18. Ask after funding decisions are made
19. Ask someone who can't make the decision
20. Ask for the wrong thing
21. Chew gum
22. Send someone who has lost faith in your cause

© 1987. McCurley & Vineyard. 101 Ways.

CHAPTER IV

UTILIZATION OF VOLUNTEERS

SATISFACTIONS TO APPEAL TO FOR PEOPLE'S INVOLVEMENT

1. Tax benefit
2. Tradition
3. Fun
4. Build resume
5. Gain experience
6. Repay perceived indebtedness
7. Opportunity to meet new people
8. Way to get acquainted with community
9. Use gifts, talents, skills
10. Way to build skills
11. Way to participate in a group
12. Earn credit for work or school
13. Get free gifts
14. Gain exposure to leaders
15. Gain leadership skills
16. Get publicity
17. Feel good
18. Help others
19. Be part of 'bigger' cause
20. Put faith into action
21. Work together as a family unit
22. Work together as a neighborhood
23. Make wrong things right
24. Promote safety
25. Act as a role model for kids
26. Cut costs for agency
27. Share own abundance
28. Change the world
29. Prevent tragedy
30. Reduce taxes
31. Advocate for human rights
32. Gain favor of people in authority
33. "Do your Part."
34. Patriotism
35. Solidarity of the family.

© 1987. McCurley & Vineyard. 101 Ways.

HOW TO MANAGE VOLUNTEERS

1. Plan carefully
    a. Set goal
    b. Involve volunteers in planning
    c. Create objectives that are specific, measurable, achievable and compatible with the overall goal
    d. Be realistic
    e. Help volunteers see where they fit in the "Big Picture"

2. Organize effectively:
    a. Create plans of action which tell who, when, how and cost of each plan
    b. Create written job designs for each job to be done
    c. Create a master time line of all jobs, who is assigned to each and when they are to be done. Give copies to everyone.

3. Staff responsibly
    a. Recruit volunteers for all jobs based on their skills, needs, motivations and experience
    b. Avoid just trying to 'fill slots' - wait to put right person in right job
    c. Train people in how to do their job - give them the information they will need for success as well as a vision of what you are doing

4. Supervise in an enabling way
    a. Help people to be successful
    b. Praise good work; correct errors immediately
    c. Catch people being good!
    d. Help people grow and discover their many good points
    e. Keep the overall goal or cause in front of people
    f. Help people feel important, included, valuable
    g. Watch for signals that people want increased responsibility
    h. Figure out what kind of recognition turns people on
    i. Be specific, brief, clear in giving instructions
    j. Be flexible
    k. Use humor to help people over rough spots
    l. Keep people on timelines
    m. Keep people informed
    n. Involve volunteers in decisions that affect them
    o. Insure that volunteers understand that there are more ways to measure success than just money: increased membership or workers, more public awareness of cause, etc.
    p. Always be fair
    q. Remind volunteers that their efforts are going to help the clients, not just the agency

© 1987. McCurley & Vineyard. 101 Ways.

HOW TO MANAGE VOLUNTEERS

5. Assess fairly
   a. Get various perspectives to assess effort
   b. Set up checkpoints in plan at which to evaluate progress
   c. When evaluating a volunteer, focus on issues not personality
   d. Soon after the fundraising effort, have an informal, relaxed evaluation. Keep the meeting positive, focusing on "What were our strengths?" and "Where did we identify opportunities for improvement?"
   e. Prepare a final report and give it to the volunteers
   f. Review goals, plans and action, and timelines as to practicality
   g. Prepare suggestions for next year's effort

6. Follow-up Promptly
   a. Recognize all volunteers involved with "thank yous" and recognition appropriate to their individual likes, needs, motivations and job responsibilities
   b. Thank all donors
   c. Keep in touch throughout the year to let volunteers and donors understand how their efforts and money are being put to use
   d. Put your feet up, treat yourself to a hot fudge sundae and enjoy the fact that you did the best you could.

REWARDS TO OFFER VOLUNTEERS

1. "Thank you"
2. Smiles
3. Name on coffee cup
4. Plaques
5. Pins
6. Badges
7. Patch
8. Organizational coffee mug
9. Photo of client helped
10. Uniform or armband
11. Satisfaction of doing a good job
12. Letter of thanks
13. Letter of appreciation to their family
14. Letter of congratulations to their employer
15. Note to clergy to tell him/her of their involvement
16. Article in newsletter of groups they belong to
17. Coupon discount booklets
18. Funny hats
19. Newspaper article
20. Free parking
21. Free meals on site
22. Positive working surroundings/conditions
23. A real job to do
24. Banquet
25. Effective supervision
26. Letter from CEO or Board President
27. Direct feedback on work done
28. Praise
29. Chance to make new relationships
30. Chance to accomplish something concrete
31. Chance to influence others
32. Opportunity to attend staff training for free
33. Special assistance if they become clients
34. Transportation
35. Reserved parking
36. Reception at home of board member
37. Attendance at board meetings as special guest
38. Chance to speak at banquet
39. Opportunity to plan future activities
40. Promotion to board
41. Input in picking type of volunteer work
42. Increased responsibility to match skills
43. Letter of job recommendation

TIPS ON WORKING WITH VOLUNTEERS

1. Treat them as an equal, vital part of your staff.
2. Have written job description for them that are clear, specific.
3. Help them understand where they "fit" in the overall picture.
4. Train them to do their work
5. Treat them fairly
6. Be open with them about problems and challenges. Don't try to "spare" them details they'll hear anyway!
7. Catch them being good! (Praise)
8. Don't offer praise when it's not deserved.
9. Utilize their gifts - don't "use" them.
10. Don't make unrealistic demands on their time, resources etc.
11. Reimburse them promptly for expenses they incur.
12. Be clear about time demands & then honor them. Don't assume that if they said they could give you 4 hours on a Saturday that they can really give you 8.
13. Listen for lame excuses of why work isn't done. It may be a cry to "get me out of this job"
14. If a volunteer is not performing the job they signed up for, even with offers of help, remove them from that job and either assign them a new, lesser responsibility one or allow them to "retire" with honors.
15. Get to know them on a personal basis and show an interest in them as a unique individual.
16. Evaluate, with their input, the work they are doing; never "evaluate" them personally.
17. Try to place them in a job where they can use their natural talents or experience so that they will be successful.
18. Celebrate their success.
19. Call them by name
20. Find out their birthday - mail them a card.
21. Never talk "down" to them. (They are probably smarter than you!)
22. Respect their other demands. (Volunteers are not put on this earth for your use alone!)
23. Encourage humor & fun while working.
24. Accept their different motivations as OK
25. Enable them to be the best they can be!

© 1987. McCurley & Vineyard. 101 Ways.

WHERE TO RECRUIT VOLUNTEERS

1. Church
2. Organizations
3. Schools (youth & adults)
4. Work
5. Over coffee (1 on 1)
6. At social events
7. Groups that are 'interested' in the same or similar issues as your cause.
8. Booths at Shopping Centers
9. At down events (parades, celebrations, etc.)
10. "Volunteer Fairs"
11. Youth Groups
12. Professional associations
13. Union meetings
14. Pre-retirement Seminars
15. conferences
16. Business meetings
17. Interest meetings
18. "Coffees" of invited; interested guests
19. Sporting events
20. Town meetings

© 1987. McCurley & Vineyard. 101 Ways.

CHAPTER V

NON-CASH RESOURCE RAISING

IDEAS FOR COST REDUCTION

1. Use of volunteer staff

2. Group purchasing of equipment and supplies

3. Inclusion in umbrella insurance arrangement

4. Community xerox machine

5. Jointly-hired staff specialists

6. Non-cash contributions of goods and services

7. Borrowing: phone books, postage machine, etc.

8. Piggybacking purchasing with businesses

9. Cooperative housing arrangements; joint leasing

10. Competitive bids for everything

11. Barter your services for goods and supplies

12. Shared transportation services

13. Shared computer facilities

14. Contest to see who can suggest best cost-cutting ideas

15. Negotiate part of local merchants newspaper ad space, free.

16. Piggyback event/cause information slips with bills, bank statements, etc.

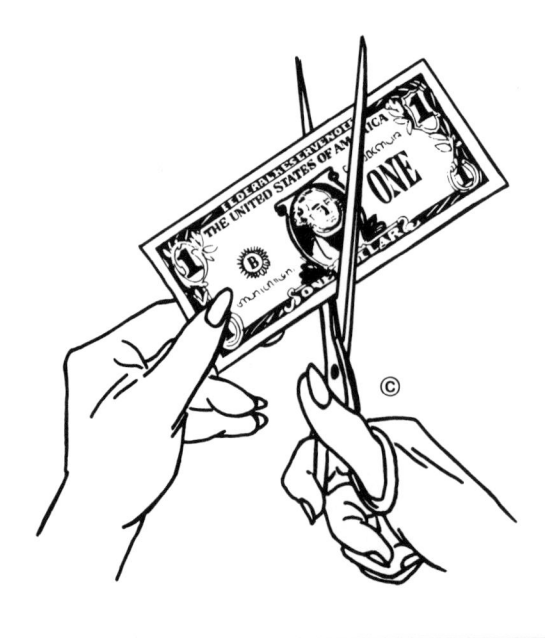

© 1987. McCurley & Vineyard. 101 Ways.

NON-CASH DONATIONS

1. Poster and brochure printing
2. Office supplies
3. Telephone
4. Computers
5. Software
6. Office furniture
7. Surplus equipment
8. Undelivered product samples
9. PR help
10. Graphic art
11. Piggyback advertising
12. Long distance access on WATS line
13. Postage meter use
14. PR stuffers in bills
15. Mailing lists
16. Market research
17. Training
18. Meeting room for board meeting
19. Training facilities
20. AV equipment
21. Production of handouts
22. PSAs

NON-CASH DONATIONS

23. Office space
24. Low-interest loans
25. Legal advice
26. Land
27. Surplus food products
28. Free soft drinks for conferences/events
29. Pencils and pads
30. Access to photocopy machine
31. Secretarial help
32. Survey design
33. Printing of brochure
34. Ads on shopping bags
35. Translators
36. Investment advice
37. Spokespersons
38. Data entry
39. Airline tickets
40. Vehicles
41. Billboards
42. Free checking/savings accounts
43. Filler ads in newspaper

SOURCES OF DONATED SERVICES

1. Accounting firms
2. Public relations firms
3. Law firms
4. Printing shops
5. Professional associations
6. Colleges
7. Businesses
8. Unions
9. Technical assistance programs
10. Government agencies
11. Retiree groups
12. Skillsbanks
13. Help Wanted Ads
14. Business and secretarial colleges
15. Vocational high schools
16. Toastmasters Clubs
17. Newspapers
18. Mailing services
19. Airlines - passenger & freight
20. Medical personnel
21. Church groups
22. Youth groups
23. Senior Citizen Homes
24. Condominium Associations
25. Civic Groups
26. Computer Clubs
27. Office Supply Businesses
28. Graphic Arts Studios
29. Cable, Educational & Network TV
30. Radio Stations
31. Film Studies classes & clubs
32. Musical Groups
33. National Guard
34. Municipal offices (police, fire, civil defense, etc.)
35. Answering Services

© 1987. McCurley & Vineyard. 101 Ways.

POTENTIAL SOURCES FOR DONATED GOODS

1. Local donated goods clearinghouses
2. Businesses moving into new quarters
3. Undelivered product samples from the Post Office
4. Banks who specialize in foreclosures
5. Lawyers who handle bankruptcies
6. Lawyers who handle estates
7. Companies having a bad sales year who have product surpluses
8. Accountants
9. Companies who are re-tooling, changing products, ending big contracts
10. Real estate management companies in areas with office space glut
11. Companies after 'end of session' merchandise sales
12. Gifts catalogue
13. "Items Wanted" ads run in newspaper
14. Community barter programs
15. Businesses who are closing
16. Government agencies facing cutbacks
17. Hotels in the banquet business: surplus meals
18. Corporate Volunteer Councils
19. "Reverse garage sales"
20. Companies promoting a new product
21. Highly competitive businesses engaging in product advertising war
22. Large non-profit
23. Donation boxes in churches
24. Corporate volunteer teams
25. School collection day
26. Large Garage Sales

© 1987. McCurley & Vineyard. 101 Ways.

CHAPTER VI

SPECIAL EVENTS

BASIC RULES FOR A SPECIAL EVENT

1. Choose the event carefully:
   a. Decide whether your bottom line is making money, generating publicity or obtaining group cohesiveness
   b. Does the type of event fit with the mission of your organization
   c. Is the type of event appropriate for your community?
   d. How is this event different from other community events?
   e. Is it within the scope of your organizational resources?
   f. Is it timed to avoid conflicts?

2. Aim at institutionalizing the event:
   a. Collect names and addresses of attendees
   b. Test the effectiveness of different marketing techniques
   c. Do post-event evaluation and review
   d. Overlap committee chairs from year to year
   e. Reward volunteers so they'll come back

3. Aim for status and fun
   a. Target "key" attendees in the community
   b. Don't be overly serious
   c. Recognize all funders publicly
   d. Look for publicity

4. Piggyback additional revenue sources
   a. Sell food and drink
   b. Sell organizational products
   c. Sell ad book space

5. Keep costs low
   a. Budget, budget, budget
   b. Look for donated resources
   c. Recruit other volunteer groups to help run the event

6. Have an escape plan
   a. Know your break-even costs
   b. Do contingency budgets
   c. Write contracts with cancellation dates
   d. Prepare a 'rain date' plan

7. Remember the prime rule:
   It is impossible to overplan a special event - someone has to know who does what to whom, when, and with what.

© 1987. McCurley & Vineyard. 101 Ways.

SPECIAL EVENT GOALS

1. Money
   a. Ticket sales income
   b. Piggyback event revenue
   c. New membership dues
   d. Names for follow-up direct solicitation
   e. Introduction to possible grant funders

2. Socialization
   a. Feeling of participation in successful event
   b. Recognition ceremony for volunteers and staff
   c. Renewal of belief in 'Cause'
   d. Reaffirmation of group endeavors: 'Band Wagon' effect

3. Public Awareness
   a. Notices in newspaper, other media
   b. Recognition by funders
   c. Exposure to attendees
   d. Contact with community leaders
   e. Recruitment of new volunteers
   f. Indication of leadership status among community groups

4. Programmatic
   a. New ideas for "Next time"
   b. Additional "experts" to help with program
   c. Enrichment of present client services

© 1987. McCurley & Vineyard. 101 Ways.

HOW TO SET THE DATE FOR YOUR SPECIAL EVENT

1. Check your timeline to assure you have enough leadtime to do a good job.

2. Check your community calendar to avoid conflicts with other groups.

3. Check school calendar to avoid conflicts

4. Check with Police or Office of Permits for any conflicts

5. Look at availability of volunteers

6. Look at availability of Special Guests

7. Look at Donors' demands

8. Read "Times Not to Schedule Special Events" in this book

9. Check your organizational plan for other projects and balance your effort against the timelines for those projects.

10. Check calendar of events for groups whose members you wish to attract as volunteers, donors, sponsors, etc.

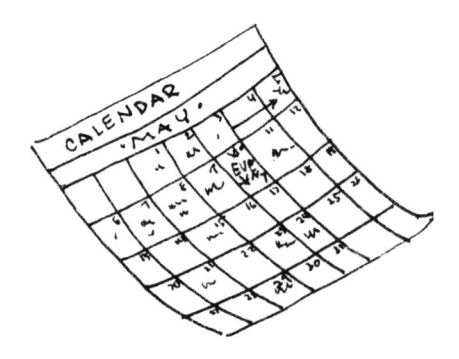

© 1987. McCurley & Vineyard. 101 Ways.

TIMES NOT TO SCHEDULE SPECIAL EVENTS

1. Religious holidays
2. Legal holiday weekends
3. School recesses if kids are part of your plans
4. State holidays
5. 1st week of school
6. Last week of school
7. Election days
8. Week before primary and general elections
9. April 15th
10. December
11. August, unless you're at the beach
12. At the same time as some other group
13. When everyone is worn out from other projects
14. During your vacation

PRICING TICKETS TO A SPECIAL EVENT

1. How much do we need to make on this event?

2. What would be a reasonable turnout size for our community?

3. What is the economic nature of our target audience?

4. How much are they used to paying for events? How much are they used to paying for our activities?

5. What 'extras' does our event have that would make people want to come?

6. What else will it cost people to attend: babysitting, tuxedo rental, etc?

7. What other ways can we generate revenue at the event?

8. What effect will a high price have on our image?

9. How quickly do we need revenue?

10. What are our break-even costs for the event?

11. How much can we gamble? How badly will we be hurt if we don't make income goals?

12. What have been the prices for similar events in the past two years?

© 1987. McCurley & Vineyard. 101 Ways.

WHAT TO PUT ON AN INVITATION TO A SPECIAL EVENT

1. Date
2. Time
3. Place
4. Price
5. Organization
6. Deadline for ticket purchase
7. Name of event
8. Event chairperson
9. Phone number for more information
10. How to respond
11. Who to make checks out to
12. Brief description of cause
13. Brief description of program for the event
14. What to wear
15. Tax deductibility status
16. Opportunity to volunteer or give contribution

SPECIAL EVENT FUNDRAISING THEMES

1. Designer Home Tour
2. VIP Golf Tournament
3. Annual Yard Sale
4. Hole-in-One Golf Tournament
5. Jail-a-thon
6. Festival Food Booth
7. Double Benefit Auction
8. Bingo
9. Celebrity Services Auction
10. Run-a-thon
11. Walk-a-thon
12. Bike-a-thon
13. Wine tasting
14. Theater Party
15. Movie Preview Party
16. Thrift Shop
17. Taste of the Town
18. Monte Carlo Night
19. Love Cup Tennis Tournament
20. Arts and Crafts Fair
21. Quilt Raffle
22. Have a Heart Dance
23. Greek Party Fraternity Dance
24. Fashion Show
25. Teen Dance
26. Community Talent Show
27. Corporate Talent Show
28. Bowl-a-thon
29. Telethon
30. World's Largest Office Party
31. Dunk-a-Director Throw
32. Community Picnic
33. Dinner ala Heart
34. Renaissance Festival
35. Pro-Am Baseball
36. Ugly Bartender Contest
37. Celebrity Cook-Off
38. Town Centennial
39. Founders Day
40. Good Samaritan Day
41. Adopt-a-thon
42. Save-a-Kid Festival
43. Senior Sock Hop
44. Wrap-a-Building Party

© 1987. McCurley & Vineyard. 101 Ways.

SPECIAL EVENT FUNDRAISING THEMES

45. Community Clean Up Day
46. Celebrity Waiters
47. Celebrity Bartender
48. Road Rally
49. Bridge Marathon
50. Ethnic Potluck Party
51. Carwash
52. Bake sale
53. White elephant sale
54. Read-a-thon
55. Rock-a-thon
56. Sale of 'care packages' to parents of college students
57. Sale of bumper stickers
58. Political Roast
59. Masquerade Ball
60. Breakfast with Santa
61. Historic tours
62. Bazaar
63. Road Rally
64. Cookbook Sale
65. Soapbox Derby
66. Used book sale
67. Treasure hunt
68. Trivial pursuit night
69. Home movies premier night
70. Children's Birthday Party
71. Birthday package from parents to kids away at school

PIGGYBACK REVENUE SOURCES

1. Food sale booths
2. Photos of attendees
3. Parking
4. Coat check concession
5. Souvenirs
6. T-shirts
7. Car wash
8. Valet parking
9. Game booths
10. Babysitting/child care
11. Ad books
12. Sale of publications
13. Gift shop
14. No Host Bar
15. Limousine transportation to and from event
16. Raffle
17. Auction
18. Art Sales
19. Dance contests
20. Sale of discount coupons
21. "Reserved Seating" Section at athletic events

CHAPTER VII

PUBLICITY

PUBLICITY

1. Publicity won't convince anyone to support a cause he/she doesn't already believe in. It is supplementary, not a complete miracle worker.

2. If you want someone to support you, you must tell them who you are, what you have to offer, what you're doing, what you've done, and what you hope to do in the future.

3. It's essential to have someone on your staff - paid or non-paid - who has mastered the principles of publicity.

4. There must be a systematized campaign designed to achieve your goals. Hit or miss won't do it.

5. A year-round publicity campaign is worth its weight in gold or chocolate, whichever you value higher.

6. Good publicity is good news.

7. If what you're doing seems 'old', put it in a new package, put a bow around it and sell it like it's brand new.

8. Two types of publicity:
    a. "For the moment" publicity - what's going on now
        1. Must be released by a certain time to be current
        2. Should tell who, what, when, where, and why
    b. "Institutional" publicity - features or background stories
        1. Tells your goals, past history, and community ties
        2. Tells who is served and how
        3. Softens up potential participants with good feelings about what you are doing. Offers credibility.

WAYS TO PROMOTE YOUR GROUP

1. Pamphlets
2. Brochures
3. Newsletters
4. Organizational Literature
5. Annual report
6. Fundraising literature
7. Flyers
8. Promos on back of bank deposit slips
9. Radio/TV spots or program segments
10. Newspaper stories
11. Messages printed on grocery bags
12. Cannisters in stores
13. Posters
14. Booth at local shopping center
15. Corporate window displays
16. Ad in yellow pages
17. Float in parade
18. Inserts in bills
19. Postal cancellation stamp
20. Banners
21. Information at library
22. Welcome Wagon information
23. Speeches to clubs
24. Talks at churches
25. Bulletin board notices
26. Piggyback advertising with local merchants
27. Inserts in newsletters

© 1987. McCurley & Vineyard. 101 Ways.

QUALITIES OF PUBLICITY CHAIRPERSON

1. Well informed about organization
2. Articulate
3. Literate
4. Meets deadlines
5. Commitment to cause/organization
6. Good public speaker
7. Persistence
8. Access to typewriter and phone. Extra credit given for camera or word processor.
9. Ability to deal positively with people
10. Previous media experience
11. Works well in crisis
12. Flexible
13. Cooperative "team player"
14. Creative

HOW TO GET PUBLICITY

1. Know what you want to publicize
2. Study the markets available to you
   a. Newspaper
      1. What do each like to print?
      2. Who is your best contact?
      3. What are their deadlines?
      4. Where can you best fit in the paper?
   b. Magazines: Which locally might publish your news?
   c. Radio and TV:
      1. Who are your contacts?
      2. What are the deadlines?
      3. What are their formats: spots; personality spots; news items; editorials; special programs; segments of programs; etc.
   d. Neighborhood outlets
      1. Posters
      2. Neighborhood newsletters
      3. Signs or banners
      4. Displays
      5. Demonstrations
      6. Poster Contest
3. Write It!
   a. Don't try to 'tell' a story to a reporter and expect it will be written by them and put in the paper.
   b. Press releases: most papers use them verbatim. You need an opening which tells everything really important; a middle which gives a further picture; a closing. Keep them short - no more than 3 paragraphs. If it needs cutting, most editors will cut off the final paragraphs, so make sure that nothing crucial is there.
   c. Always put your name, address, group name and home or business phone number at the top of all submitted material.
   d. Letters: this is a sales tool to convince editor to print subsequent story. Keep it brief, to the point. Use 3 paragraphs: the first a teaser; the second to whet the appetite; and the third to convey what you have in mind.
   e. Photo captions: pictures usually get printed, especially if they are timely and show local people or events. Write the caption carefully and get the names right.
   f. Public Service Announcements: Copy must be timed. Standard spots are 10 seconds (approximately 25 words for radio; 20 for TV); 20 second, or 60 seconds.
4. Use of the Telephone
   a. Know what you want to say.
   b. Never underestimate the position or power of the person you're talking with.
   c. Phone to follow-up on a release or letter you've sent.
   d. Phone to tell the 'right' person on the paper (whoever is responsible for getting your story printed) that an article is coming.

© 1987. McCurley & Vineyard. 101 Ways.

FREE PUBLIC RELATIONS HELP

1. Market analysis and research: agency, publics, community

2. Mailing list

3. Local media list

4. Demographic analysis of community

5. Design of posters and brochures

6. Piggyback advertising

7. Spokesperson training

8. Help in PSA production

9. Referral/introduction to media contacts

10. Use of AV equipment

11. Advice on ad placements

© 1987. McCurley & Vineyard. 101 Ways.

TIMELINE FOR SPECIAL EVENT PUBLICITY

1. 6-10 Weeks Prior to Event: Mail invitations or announcement.

2. 4 Weeks Prior: Start placement of public service announcements.

3. 3 Weeks Prior: Place newspaper announcement of event.

4. 2 Weeks Prior: Try to get news feature story about event or persons involved in event.

5. 1-2 Weeks Prior: Get announcements in weekly and community newspapers.

6. Day before: Finalize coverage of event itself. Arrange for volunteer escorts for press representatives.

7. Week After: Plant stories of results of event. Send thank yous for press coverage.